T0196699

STILL TRYING
to FIND *The*
Light

MS. KIM

authorHOUSE®

AuthorHouse™
1663 Liberty Drive
Bloomington, IN 47403
www.authorhouse.com
Phone: 833-262-8899

Published by AuthorHouse 05/06/2022

ISBN: 978-1-6655-5913-3 (sc)
ISBN: 978-1-6655-5912-6 (e)

Print information available on the last page.

Any people depicted in stock imagery provided by Getty Images are models, and such images are being used for illustrative purposes only.
Certain stock imagery © Getty Images.

This book is printed on acid-free paper.

Because of the dynamic nature of the Internet, any web addresses or links contained in this book may have changed since publication and may no longer be valid. The views expressed in this work are solely those of the author and do not necessarily reflect the views of the publisher, and the publisher hereby disclaims any responsibility for them.

CONTENTS

INTRODUCTION

This book is about a female who have went through a lot of tribes and tribulations as a teen a little bit about what she overcame as an adult she was so young searching for love in the wrong spots that she did what ever to keep on with a relationship she had for almost seven years until she decided to depart from the relationship after having two beautiful daughters when she turned 20 she decided that she would move and find an apartment later on she then moved in to her apartment where she later then began to have problems she was trying to move out the apartment but they seem to get intense and she really had to move her life was like a living hell growing up in north Philadelphia where all the drugs are where people are getting killed left and right just to be in a situation where she like she would never get out of but in the book four years later she met her a fine ass chocolate and he sure helped through a whole lot second book she writes will continue with that story on how else they met I hope that you find this book entertaining also might have you a little teary but also it will teach you something this book is not bashing or harassing or disrespecting anyone it's simply explains how even if you go through a hard time either relationship with a man or family member that you still can over come your flaws.....

The beginning of My misery 16 years of life has begun. Well let's just say I'm getting ready for job Corp because my school ain't want me anymore, do to my poor behavior in class including cutting school, fighting and smoking weed you know how teen girls do we just want to smoke do what we want with no self respect our minds are every where because there's no rules at least we think we don't have rules because there's no one giving us discipline or don't even know how to because we so busy raising our self and being hot in the pants we think we know it all I always ended up making the wrong decisions.

Let me finish telling you the rest on how I end up having to leave for jobCorp, me and my mom was fighting because she was trying to make me come in at seven at night, mind you I'm 16 why not 10 or 11 i asked her "mom why do I have to come in so early it's only 7 pm? Her reply was "Kim stop fucking asking me why you have to come in at seven what you think you fucking grown that you can come in at all kinds of late hours? "why your ass ain't stay in the foster home with your fucking foster mom you came back to get on my fucking nerves. All I said was why so early she yelled at me and "boom" there she goes dragging me by the hair hitting me kicking me biting and so much more, I got so upset I start hitting her punching her in her face I simply blanked out.

I left out her house to the neighbor house because I was scared she might have killed me. she called my DHS worker mrs. Tanner y told her loudly on the phone "Mrs. tanner please come get this little girl out my house before I kill her she hit me I'm her mother take her back where ever I don't care just please get her out. What's so crazy about this whole thing was that my aunt Vanity was there that day she watched and after I finished before I even left she was pissed she try calling me and my mom out I ain't scared of her or no one on planet earth it's different with her she practically raised me and she was trying to pretty much adopt me but my mom wasn't trying to she was all in for the social security I was getting SSI seizures I had as a kid, I know was wrong but understand me though, she put me through hell I'll tell you that on my second chapter but right now we at chapter one. so any how I'm packing up getting all my stuff my aunt bought me all of my stuff my mom ain't bought me nothing for jobcorp, well everything is packed and ready to just leave my aunt walks in my room and says "Kim you are about to make me cry oh my god, "but maybe it's for the better I wish I could of got your custody but I can't because I don't have my own house". So then as I walked out my mom door I didn't even bother looking back I got in the van and left to the greyhound to leave for job Corp oh yeah it's in Vegas.

CHAPTER

1

So I finally get to the greyhound waiting for the bus to let us in got my bus ticket I'm just thinking what is job Corp like what them people about in Vegas because that's one weird ass name sounds like a weird country place with a bunch of trees like dam I'm nervous because my hair is a mess it's straight with bangs and sure feels weird, people might start laughing and I might get mad I don't know I'll find out when I get to Vegas. It's 10 minutes later and now I'm on the bus these chairs ain't so bad it's cold in here and there's a lot of people in here but who cares there's tv and movies and I'm falling asleep zzzz.. until the bus gets there because the ride is seven hours and ain't nobody trying to be up the whole ride unless I'm getting some dam food.

Now I'm woke and we made it finally to a stop for a break to go to the bathroom and to get some food so when I got off a girl approached me her name was heaven she was real cool we walked to the bathroom talked came out she asked if I can buy her something to eat because she ain't have no money on her got it we ate laughed about my hair style I had. we got back on the bus to make our way to Pittsburgh I was so ready to have my stuff in a closet and take a shower so I can go to sleep. One more hour and we will be in vegas I wonder how many of us on this bus going to jobcorp.

I made it to Vegas hours later to get right back on another bus but a cheese bus this time and it was about two more girls that I remember of which was Sarai and Natalie they were cool to we laughed about my hair to lmao I called my self Mexican that day hey no offense but I could favor them a little.

Lol here's one I think this was two days before I faught my mom back to talking about Sarai and Natalie the two I told you I met in the cheese bus. So we finally made it to job Corp we grabbed all of our luggage took it in side this building security guards were out in front when we finally got inside there was two ladies they asked about trades names showed us to our temporary dorm rooms Sarai and heaven was in one room Natalie in another one with some girl don't remember the name. Made it to my room it was kind of small but I had a roommate she was older than me in her middle twenties her name was jasmine she was cool she always dressed really nice let's be real and sexy to she had sexy clothes on all the time except when it was time for class. We had to share a bathroom I didn't really like it but hey it was what it was as long as she was clean.

So two nights later they moved everyone out the building in to another building and new dorm rooms that's when me heaven, Natalie and sarai was in the same room it was ok but I ain't really like it all like that it was always so awkward because they would speak to me but not all like that in the beginning I'm guessing they must of thought I was weird because I was to quiet or that I was a punk I wasn't I was just always to my self and who ever started a fight with me or try to hit me I'll hit them back that's different but in this case I was in jobcorp I ain't really know no body. So we all finally went to sleep to wake up super early I was beat seriously.

It was 6:00am sharp and some dam girl knocked on the door talking about "Detail time wake up. I'm like "ayo what the fuck did I get in to I thought I was in boot camp some where I'm thinking like am I in the right place I thought I was taking up CNA. so I get up put my shoes on and the worst day begins in jobcorp I open up the door and the girl said clean the bathroom gave me a mop and broom like yo I be dam if I'm coming here to clean some dam bathrooms. I start cleaning the bathroom so they won't try kicking me out after I finished I went back in the room to get my clothes ready to go to my first class then got in the shower. 15 minutes goes by here goes the guard or what ever she was "hurry up in the shower we ain't got all day other people need to shower, so I grabbed my towel to get out I go in to the room put my hygiene stuff on got dressed stepped out to go down to the cafeteria the breakfast was not really good at all it tasted like precooked food I use to sit with the three girls talk a little then they start talking I just was always quiet unless they said something to me.

I made it to my second class which felt so weird because the people in the class was weird I think I was cool with one or two of them who weren't weird I can't remember their names. Four hours later I was done class and on to lunch didn't really eat lunch I walked around with the girls instead. I went to GED class and met my teacher she was so nice and helpful she corrected me every time I was wrong on one of my essays on the computer not the answer just telling me to go over it thank god I ain't give no names because some body probably would of said something lol just kidding it's 3:30pm I was done class and on my way to my dorm to change my clothes to go outside for a little or down stairs when I was walking with the girls Natalie wanted me to get a number for her but I was bitching lmao she wanted me to play like I wanted him but it was all her so I decided to play it off got his number gave it to her or I think he wrote it on my hand 2 weeks go by me and the guy and girls all hanging out busting it up laughing Natalie started talking to him telling him it was her idea and I believe a week later this girl knocking in our room talking about "where is she tell her I want to speak to her. so I'm like" what the girl come in the room talking about bitch why you talking to my man I'm like "who your man? She says "josh I been with him before you even came here I told her "ain't no body talking to your man or worried about him like what ever then went back about my business and she left the room.

Hey good morning woke up on a Saturday morning hanging around with the girls we was getting ready for breakfast so that we can go in to this hang out lobby place they have in here heaven comes in and asked was I ready, "hey Kim you ready so we can go downstairs to get breakfast? I respond back to her "yes I'm ready wonder what them cute guys down there looking like, maybe I'll find a cute one. Heaven looking at me like "girl I know but relax your self we about to go down stairs. So as we walking down the steps to open the door I see this guy he is so fine and I just can't stop stairing at him but the worst part is this guy have a girlfriend but I'm still taking a sneak peek at him while I walk down the hall 😔 his lips are so juicy, his eyes are hazel, and he just was perfect for the moment. We in the cafeteria getting our

Breakfast I ain't have no choice but to put something in my stomach even if it wasn't all great right after I finished my breakfast I went to the lobby where every body can play pool video games and watch tv it was chill but dam all these guys was in my face and I'm like well okay I met this other guy he was cool but I couldn't click with him like I felt with this guy I seen in the hall way. So anyways i end up buying ice cream and sitting down to watch a movie and talk with the girls until 11:00 that was our curfew to go upstairs on the weekends that shit was crazy they tell you when to wake and sleep but thank god on the weekends we can sleep in because I refused to miss out on a nap.

It's a 11:00pm and made it back to my room took another shower put my pjs on and went in the room I didn't really sleep because they like staying up almost all night sometimes they watch stuff on their phone or eating snacks because there wasn't really much to do some of us was young and we couldn't go out to clubs so we be in our rooms and I be relaxing until Monday so I can start class all over again ugh can't wait until all of this is over and I'm older so I ain't got to deal with this crap in here, because god knows these females in here are so dam nasty so remember that day I talked about having to mop and sweep this Detail time bullshit so while I'm cleaning the bathrooms tell me how there was shit on the wall of the bathroom like oh hell no my ass went in the hall way called this guard lady and told her I'm not cleaning that bathroom and she was like "Excuse me what was that"? So I responded back "I'm not cleaning no body bathroom with shit on the walls that ain't mine like nah that's fucking nasty." So while I'm telling her she's yelling "who done put their nasty ass on the wall like come on y'all ain't come here to be putting shit on walls that's nasty and I'm going to find out. back to my regular day going to sleep I definitely need to be up and out the dam door so I ain't got to worry about that shit again. five minutes go by people spreading a rumor that it was me I might looked weird but ain't no body wasn't about to be putting shit on the wall though I didn't really care what people thought because half of them was weird.

Good morning I'm up and ready to start my day it's Sunday so I have to make this fun before class tomorrow so I picked out this nice little outfit some shorts and a black shirt not nice but you know what I mean comfortable so I can walk around the campus. It's official been a month that I been here it's ok I'm just so ready to start my trade so I can get out of here and hopefully find a job and do something with my self since I know me and my mom not talking. recently I even found out that she still had my disability check on and lied to these people that I was on vacation like I was never going back to her abusive ways so I let that be because I know god going to punish her for the dumb choices she made, not knowing how to be a parent is a dam shame you really lied just so you can have money but have not yet to send me anything. I'm dressed heading to the door while going outside look who I see Dwayne that fine light skin built brotha so he's in front of the door talking to some guy name mike which was Sarai brother faith was conversating with them as well while I walked with my home work minding my business and faith walks up and says "Kim mike friend want you his name Dwayne, I said "ok tell him to come to the table so I'm guessing he heard what I said and walked up to me sat down in front of me and was like where you from I told him "well cutie I'm from north Philly and I'm really a fall back girl, where you from? "don't you got a girlfriend? name lily or some shit like that don't want to get you in trouble. "Girl ain't nobody getting in trouble me and her broke up and she was leaving any way so what am I suppose to do wait on her nah ma I'm cool maybe we can get to know each other." And go out a little bit and maybe be something. So I looked at him laughed, I replied "boo you never know what might can happen but let's take it slow we can go for a walk or something. Do you want to go for a walk not all of us just me and you he said "yeah we can that's cool, make sure you finish that homework.

So as I began to do my home work, it changed from me doing my homework to him finishing it for for me I was like you really ain't have to do that, he said "beautiful I'm just trying to help I even laughed about it the cutest thing a guy have done so far, I asked him where was he from he responds "I'm from west Philadelphia have you ever been down that way? I respond back "yeah me and my foster mom grand daughter use to go up 52nd and market with her friends but that's about it, "im from north as I said before and I'm real lay back and humble. While we walk he touches my waste and we walk to the back of the campus where they have chairs and we kept on talking but lawd it's getting hot because as soon as we was about to get up he kisses me then laughed and said I see you tomorrow beautiful I'm going to play ball sorry for such a short chill time. shit I was sixteen what was I suppose to do, I already thought I was grown while walking to open the door to make my way upstairs because as usual had to get ready for dinner, I saw this new girl boo loving with some dude I went to the other doors to go up stairs. I don't even know is she seen me I hope she didn't If she did she just thought my ass was weird.

So I didn't bring up the day me and him was in the back I mean you knew we sat down but we was kissing like we was about to fuck my head was every where since he kissed me I'm all in my head thinking dam his lips was so juicy and soft I'm up in my room just letting my head float but guess it's time to wake up out my freak bag and take my ass to the cafeteria for dinner. I need to see what the girls are doing and if they are ready to go back down stairs open up my room door making it to the other side of the dorm rooms and heaven was already in the hall way saying "hey niece what you doing"? You ready to go see your boo again I think he might be down there for dinner

I start blushing and responded

"I hope he is downstairs, tell me how when we was in the back of the building he kissed me". Heaven respond "dam girl he done got you all butterflied up he done kissed you niece? ok niece don't start switching up ditching us. "girl please I'm not about to be doing all of that for some guy nope not happening but I will have my moments alone with him just saying lmao I might get some dick. Heaven respond "Kim you sure is freaked out you might just get some. "I know you ain't talking you might got something planned to ms adopted aunt lol we acted like we adopted each other first it's niece or maybe she calls me sis.

We finally made it to the cafeteria I for got about our other friend Brandon he was cool he was a fall back dude always had our asses laughing he stay trying to play some body but he was cheerful but I just took my ass to the table with the girls and just waiting on some other girls so we can get on the line to eat because I won't lie I'm hungry hopefully I see him again today. I really had a good day with him that day he really brought a smile to my face I haven't smiled in such a long time. As I make my way to the line I seen my sexy Dwayne just walking up to me talking about "dam baby you stalking me or am I to fine that you keep finding me?

"boy please all I was doing was getting in the line so I can go get my food to sit down that's all lol you funny you just want me to see you again just say that then. He looked at me and laughed I kept on moving up to get my food after grabbing it I walked to my table so Dwayne yells "come sit with me. So I told the girls "im going to sit with him don't worry ain't no body switching up just want to see what's up with him and dam don't it feel like a year it's only been three months that we been here.

me and him sitting on the table he eating and I'm just sitting picking at my food because I was to shy to even dare eat in front of him, I didn't know how to act He looked at me crazy and laughed and said "so you just going to pick at your food and not eat what you shy?"

yes I'm shy mr Dwayne how about turn your face and I might just can eat because the way people looking at me they probably think I'm crazy. "Because I'm not eating lmao. He laughed and said "girl stop acting shy and eat I'm not going to bite unless you want me to but besides that how old are you if you don't mind me asking? "I'm 16 and how old are you since you asking me questions and acting like you trying to make me your girl? He responded back "I'm 18 the age ain't no different just two years apart and what if I wanted you to be my girl is that a problem? "who said I said it's a problem and be yours maybe but not to fast ok we just met and I'm taking shit really slow.

"Girl I know you trying to take it slow chill we chill go on dates and what not and go from there." but I'm about to get going cutie about to go with my boys to the woods and smoke some bud do you smoke? "I respond now of course I smoke but since I'm 16 they ain't about to let me leave and come back late. his reply was "dam shawty wish you can come but I see you tomorrow ok is that cool? "yes that's cool I'm about to get going to me and the girls going back up to the door rooms to chill might just take a selfie and send it to you is that cool with you? Now I'm just being a straight smart ass just because you said it first. "of course I want picture cutie ok then i see you.

"hey heaven you missed me yet I was with my little boo but what we doing when we get up there ain't the guard giving snacks out at like 7pm? She responded back "yeah the guard definitely is so we need to make it up there and then I guess I can put a movie in the little lounge upstairs and I might call my boo. "oh ok so let's make our way up to the dorm and relax I'm sleepy where's Natalie? "girl I'm right behind you I was calling both of y'all but y'all was to far to hear me. "awww boo my bad we was stuck talking about how I was sitting with my boo today at the cafeteria I was blushing girl I couldn't even eat, "I'm going in my room real quick to change my clothes so we can get this movie started. I walked to my room open the door and sat down on my bed getting ready to put some red lipstick

I hope he like this picture because I'm sure feeling myself and I know I'm looking cute and my lips looking juicy I definitely can't control my self I'm feeling my self.

He finally text back got me over here not knowing if I want to come out this room or not because he sure do speak freaky lawd I'm loving it. I know the girls are going to knock on my door just to see if I'm ready to go to the tv room, so I should just make my way out the door so I can watch me a movie and relax my self. Closing the door and walking to get some snacks then movie begins, dam this vending machine got so much snacks I don't know what I want is so much snacks to pick heaven walking behind me "niece what you getting to snack on? "I don't even know yet maybe some chips will be ok a soda

Makes it even better, are you getting something out the ice cream machine I'm thinking about getting that to need something cold while watching a movie

"yeah I might get that to so you still texting your boo niece? "Auntie you already know I did I send him a picture of me girl his messages be freaky.

"what about you and your boo I seen y'all last night before coming up all kissing I'm surprise he ain't eat you out lmao. she responded "girl I might just do that tomorrow it's girls night don't feel like

Doing all that tonight, "plus we about to be watching some good ass movies. We made it to the tv room so we can watch this movie and I can just be texting my boo. I respond "oh ok you love your niece today girl I feel you I'm doing the same because there's so much I have to do this week in class I think we start our trades in another week, "What trade was you taking up I know I'm taking up certified nursing assistant. "well girl I'm taking up Culinary so that I can be cooking all kind of meals I'm trying to be on point when it comes to my meals for my future man.

Two hours later we still in the tv room the guard came in and said "come on girls it's time to shut it down you have to get up in the morning at 7am to do your details. So I got up made my self out the door walking to move texting Dwayne fine ass to see if he still up because dam he been on my mind I couldn't even concentrate on the movie all I kept think about was him kissing me on my lips giving me that sexual eye contact mmm... just the thought of him stroking me so hard making my pussy wet. Getting my pajamas out and putting them on so I can get my self up in the morning I'm glad I took an shower I'm not about to clean a dam thing I'm walking out the dam door because after that nasty shit some body pulled off in that dam bathroom putting shit on the wall I was done the guard can say what she want I don't even give a fuck because I know for a fact she wouldn't clean no body shit off no wall and I know I'm not doing it so she better get someone else to do that shit unless she gotta better detail like cleaning hall ways and trash.

This my picture first thing in the morning while waking up and forgetting he let me hold his hat I picture mailed him told him "don't forget you let me hold your hat don't I look good with it on boo? So while waiting for his text I'm still trying to get my self ready for class I feel so lazy I'm still exhausted after sleeping late plus the guard woke us up to make us go right in our room but I didn't care because I was already about to get up because I need it to get up be ready to head out the door, I really didn't feel like going to class all I wanted to do was sleep texting Dwayne almost the whole night I can not wait until this weekend I might just give it up. It's been five months I need some he better be pulling my hair plus smacking this ass.

I love freaky shit for example i love my hair pulled, ass smacked, thumb in the butt, pussy ate Let's not forget the best part of sex which is whispering in the ears when me and him get freaky I want it to feel like it was my last time even having sex. I can't wait for the day to be over i might have to masturbate, focus on what me and Dwayne going to be doing over the weekend I'm excited I might be nervous I don't know.

Class is almost over I might just take a nap first before I plan on doing anything heaven was going to be busy spending time with her boo I can dig it because I'm going to be doing the same this weekend I'm going to chill with him today but we ain't really going to do nothing besides talk when I should make him buy me some snacks from the machine plus I needed help with my math homework me and math don't get along long division is hard the only way I knew how to solve those math problems was for someone to do one of the math questions and then explain why they solved it that's maybe the easiest way for me.

Class is really done with all this talking I be doing the day goes by I'm always thinking about new things maybe plan my goals so when I leave out of here I'm settled I don't really have no where to go my mom don't want me, my dad to strict for me to be forced to go to places I don't want to go or he just a loud ass person with an attitude.

I decided that it's been a little while since I spoken to my mother let me try speaking to my aunt let's see what she got to say maybe she can tell me how my mom doing. so the phone is ringing for about two seconds and she picks up "hello who is this? "Hey mom it's me Kim I'm calling from the job corp office they let you make phone calls, I'm calling from their phone because my cell phone was cut off and I had no other way to call I wanted how my mom was doing? I'm thinking in my head like what would my aunt say and is it any good or bad news I need to head about my mother allah help.

"yeah I spoke to your mom you already know what she up to always in some shit talking shit I had to curse her the fuck out telling people I fuck men in the ass like dam who business is that and she brought up the dude I did do something to. "She just don't know what to do with her self at all running her mouth about my business

I think your mom still have your SSI on she lied all I heard was "she is on vacation coming back she also eats off a feeding tube. I could not believe that she would say some crazy shit like that but you know karma going to kick her in the ass watch.

Looking back in my phone this picture was when I was placed in my foster home almost around the same time my mom clown Ass son which is my brother, he decided to make a stupid decision. Him and his friends decided to do something so dumb that he had to go in to prison for a couple years the thought of that happening really broke my heart he's my brother

Back to talking about this picture, I looked like I was about to go for a lawyer position I wish a shawty like me was in a position like that. I would not be in Philadelphia because this city is really whiled I mean every where the same but I'm sure not in no country place you going to really hear about any killing you might hear more birds and crickets if anything. I wonder what my boo is doing ain't speak to him all day forreal I really miss him I don't even know why I'm feeling these bubble guts every time I think of him, I just turn my back about to smack somebody when I realized it was my teacher she had me laughing her first reaction was "Kim what you thought you saw a ghost?? "no I just don't really like no one sneaking up on me like that I was turn the other way and ain't even hear or feel no body but hands touched me sorry about that.

"sorry about that Kim lol I thought you were going to sneak me for a second, I just wanted to tell you that you are passing all your exams and almost done your high school diploma class. Now you know I was excited to hear my teacher tell me I'm passing so that I can get out her class have my diploma plus celebrate my birthday, I'm sure I'll be done by my birthday maybe I'll get my self a cake that will be nice. "I'm so happy thank you I'll see you tomorrow I might need help with my essay. "I'll be glad to help you.

Fifteen minutes went by I'm walking outside to the other side of the building to make my way to my new class which Is gym wondering who in that class hopefully not one of them bitches who look at you like you crazy, because believe me I know how to defend my self what's crazy is no one will understand my personality hello why else will they tell you to watch out for the quiet ones because ima let you talk but just don't touch me because when I start crying that means move, I'm going to make sure I'm humble.

I walked in to the gym class everybody just start staring at me I'm wondering what the hell did they lost because staring at me was not solving their problem. One guy looks at me his first words were "dam girl how you doing? my name is T-pain where you from? I looked at him the first thing I said to him was "first of all the way you approach a female ain't no where near attractive second of all you aren't my type but last but not least I came here to have gym class not booty calls. I walked off saw group of girls see what they were doing, they have this girl name Layla she look weird looking i believe she is in one of my classes math I believe she so fucking weird she even sound like she came from Alabama.

Thinking about it makes me laugh she keep staring at me just like them guys playing ball, she walking towards me and asked me "hey where you from my name is Layla I'm from around here I seen you been staring at me all week since we started math class together, is there a problem? I looked at her respond back "girl it's called they're my eyes I stare where I please at any giving time who the fuck do you think you talking to? "wait I'm lost why are you popping out on me like that I only asked you one question because you don't sound like you from up here you sound different. "im from Philly I guess Philly people sound more different than Pittsburgh people sorry if I snapped out I get offended really fast don't know why.

"you sure do snap out fast I guess because you a city kid and I'm like the saying "COUNTRY" kid but once you get to know me I'm really bomb. So I looked at her I wanted to laugh so bad but I managed to hold it in because I ain't want god punishing me for my sin, shit I had enough sins in me I just try my best to do better keep my aunt Mara happy showing her I can change my life. "yeah that's just me I'm not use to people asking so much questions about me, I'm to quiet for a million questions but what's it like up here? "Well Pittsburgh so wild girl we be getting it Giggy I'll show you around one day I'm about to go get me a pop and chips. "ok see you around, I headed

My way to find something to do in the gym since I have nothing else to do until I get to my room.

Gym class is finally over now I can take my ass up to my dorm wonder what my boo up to I ain't hitting him up until he do I don't do all that joe shit with niggas I be dam. Plus what I look like being thirsty he should be showing me how much he want me, I can't keep showing him shit not today not ever I'm to way to smart for all of that. Five minutes goes by and my phone start ringing and guess who was calling my boo I'm about to pick up "hello? Wassup boo how was your day? He responded "nothing boo I been playing ball with the boys and about to go to the mall so I can get me a nice lay to wear so when I see that sexy ass Friday. "dam boo it's like that you about to look nice for me? I'm impressed by that best believe Friday I will be showing skin.

"you acting like you about to be getting in this hmmmm. "don't do all that boy I will drop those drawls, he responded back "I don't think you want to do that girl I will beat that pussy up you will be limping. Not only would I have you limping you will fall more in love with me I promise you, lol you are so funny me fall in love nah I don't think so I don't fall in love y'all players and trust me I ain't no where near dumb what makes you think ima fall for your line you use for every female you try to fuck. But all in reality I want him to fuck me so good I cum I'm young I want to just have fun I'm in jobcorp but I'm also careful because I ain't got time for no dam disease, and at that who knows if I will feel comfortable with him touching me after all the shit I went through being in a foster home having a good foster mom but also the fact that I decided to he dumb go to a guy house to see what sex felt like and when I was laying down he was trying to stick it in but I told him no it hurt but his dumb ass ain't care he flipped me cover my mouth and fucked me from the back I hate that memory I hate all my memory as a kid but im telling you that on the next chapter of my second book.

"girl I'm not going to go rough on you I'm going to be real slow fam you so mean why all that, I was just responding to what you said you a fisty one. "I'm not being mean I'm just saying you couldn't handle me even if you said you can but we will definitely see about it love I love feeling good strokes I want to be dripping. As I get ready to walk away and wait for tomorrow for the big day Friday here comes weezy ass kissing on me dam that shit just felt so right his lips all soft just the thoughts that run in my head, "see you later boo going upstairs getting ready for this shower and rest I ain't coming down today all I want to do is sleep and get ready for tomorrow.

"Uhhhhhh this stretch feels so good about to get ready for this very special moment and taking advantage of being here with his fine ass and finally letting him hit these cheeks, I need a relieve with all the stress I'm going through shit I don't think I can take no more dam stress being in foster homes, court, group homes and then going back home with my mom I just want to finish my trade and work and he'll no I don't want no dam kids right now not at this point." Hey girl wake up time to get dress faith said I responded "girl I'm already woke for that dick hahahahaha what are you doing today "nothing besides chill with my boo and maybe eat well I see you later then because we got a lot to do with our boos. So I'm getting dress and out the door and walking downstairs and I see my boo he looking at me like he trying to eat me up I'm sure that I said that line already some where in the chapter but that's my favorite line sorry can't help my self this is my way of speaking can't change it so any-whom he's coming omg let me get my fucking self together I'm tripping ok fixing my hair making sure I'm looking good ok so now here he comes "hey babe you looking good you ready for me we can walk and talk if you want no need to all the extra if you don't want to. He was so sweet about it but please who the fuck he thought he was talking to a dumb ass nah I know your ass want some pussy he swear he can hold his self let's begin the game.

"so where are we so call walking to sir lmao I know you ain't slick lmao let's see who going to start the first move I'm sure it would be you watch. Girl if I want to touch you I would have been touched you but I'll wait for you to make the first move so you will feel comfortable and we only taking a walk and if you want we can go to the movies or I can show you around up here up to you love u less you trying to be nasty. "girl you always thinking someone just trying to fuck I ain't stop fucking with my ex to try and play you I did it because I saw potential love, feel me so chill. Boy nobody saying that I just ask 21 questions because I don't trust no one income from a fucked up place so I don't really know how to be nice unless I have to be and want to be, you also have to deserve my niceness.

"I came to jobcorp to get my shit together because my mother threw me out we fought I think I told you that maybe I remind you I been through to much pain mileages at 5, my mom locked me in rooms slapped, kicked, punched, also she bit me so I said fuck it I don't know want to go back to placement or foster homes I'll do jobcorps I loved my foster mom Ms. Laly but being at her house was to much being up late because my foster sisters were loud I loved them but dam they were loud and some bad ass kids always trying to fight me and I was right at them and then they got used to me but I was ready to go back home with my mom to see if she changed and boom that's when shit went down hill and now I'm here. "Dam, you been through some shit nah I promise to things slowly with you sounds like you been through to much pain you can't bare no more of it I won't hurt you just trust me okay. Ok I'll try being nice only because I see you some what feel where I come from with me and my body and feelings.

We continued to walk and talk about life he told me he been through a lot but he never really said where he was from, never really bothered to ask him niether it wasn't really my business but I also wasn't trying to get my ass killed by no crazy ass dude and that's real shit. "so Kim what do you like to do for fun? Well I don't really do much or never really went out my mom was always bugging and yelling all the time telling me to get my ass in or I couldn't go out with none of my friends but if I ever get the chance to go out I'll go bowling or shopping little shit to get by while being in here feeling like I'm locked up with people in a group home or juvenile. "yeah I feel what you saying me and my home boys always out going to the mall movies shit I sneak in bars shit there's a lot you can do up here one day I'll take you around so you can see what it's like it's almost like being in Philly but they speak different I'm sure you know that because you done spoke to chicks who from up here. Yeah some girl name Lelani.

she done told me a couple things about up here I ain't really planning on going out or doing anything crazy because it ain't like I can do much I'm only six teen. "Oh yeah you a young shawty I mean I always got away with going to places maybe you don't know how to present your self like you an adult, "I am mature what lmao you are to funny just because I'm not of age doesn't mean I don't present my self like an adult I just act like my self and that's all it is to it. "I don't have to act like none of these girls in here I'm really laid back let me find out you trying to cause trouble with me. "girl ain't no body starting no trouble I'm just saying you acting as if you can't get some dress up shoes and a dress to go out and act older girl you better stop playing with me and go out with me be my date to the movies, take you to the restaurant after the movies and come back so wassup. "Ard you just have to let me know and I make a move and what kind of transportation do they have up here?" they have some where buses that come by here, shit I don't care better than being here and eating that nasty ass food and I would love to know different shit around here.

"you will trust me ain't nothing to figure out especially here in Pittsburgh it's like being in philly but houses are different and it's mostly hills, one day we can go to the market and walk back a couple of miles. "pause miles from where not me with all them bushes and wild animals is you crazy? "lmao what you scared of trees and dark? Girl you better stop playing you ain't going to get attacked by no dam animal I'm right here chill it's going to be fun we going to laugh smoke and maybe drink a little. We can go to the market and walk back or we can catch the bus. So my dumb ass decided to agree and we set it up for 7:30.

"Dam girl you looking good where you going said heaven and Natalie, "girl I'm going out with Dwayne fine ass girl he told me to go out with him so i told him ok he talking about taking me to the movies and out to eat so I said ok why not. "Girl I know that's right you go get your boo and have fun I'm about to go downstairs with heaven and Sarai, "well tell heaven I see her when I get back girl might just get some ugh I need it one thing I don't give a fuck about is what people got to say I'm young and having fun. "girl go have fun and fuck what people got to say they not you or helping you so there for go get you some dick if you want it "hahahahahaha." I will I'm not worried about no body but me I just want a peace of mind away from here it's to closed in and I need to breath it ain't like my family worried about me I don't even fuck my mom like that she never even thought about me since I been here not a call no nothing she ain't even think about paying my cellphone so yes I need some fresh air.

"Girl go do you every one doesn't have a perfect mom and maybe one day she will change who knows, just go have fun and forget about everyone else. "Awwww thanks boo I will I guess I see you later then because girl I do not need to be late for what ever it is about to go down. "Hey wassup girl you look so beautiful thank you for coming I thought you weren't going to come. "boy please I was ready just was talking to the girls, where are we going any ways? "we going to the movies then chill that's all ain't trying to do nothing girl. Well I didn't say anything about something happening I was asking where we was going that's all ain't nothing popping unless you wanted that lmaooo.

Now as I get down to the very last or at least some of the parts of my life when my next page comes in I promise people won't take their eyes out well back to me and him before this story done I have to finish where me and Wayne started. On that day we went out he took me out to eat, fresh breeze, drink and smoke he had his little homies that knew a spot in the woods man them woods be mad crazy you hear everybody fucking on each side of the trees it didn't make no dam sense." Omg yo people crazy they really out here fucking omg they is crazy if a animal bite their ass they done. "lmaooo Kim this my normal chill spot if it ain't in the woods it's up the hill l, I got to get you back soon because they have people your age on a curfew. "Dwayne I been knew about that please I am not a baby I can walk my self I got this I'm getting ready to walk up before it gets to late I'm really tired and fried the food was great by the way I had fun I guess I see you around or another day it's up to you. "yeah ima see you around girl hopefully tomorrow we can go to the cafeteria together.

Well what can I say so far I been having fun with him it's been great but my mind is all over the place the fact that my mom nor my father even thought to send me things I don't have money like that in here it's crazy you get 25 allowance like wtf is that it ain't enough for panties or bras, just so lost but I'll get to the next chapter with that I will start by saying that my next book will be coming soon just want to make it interested for everyone especially who been in my shoes

CHAPTER

2

I told you all I would be telling you about my next chapter well here it goes I am now a mother I graduated jobcorps believe it or not I end up moving with Dwayne to his grandma house let me tell you in the beginning it was all peaches and creams they was acting nice talking nice but when I first had my daughter sai everything changed his grandma was ignorant no disrespect because she's an elderly person but she knew what she was doing she was telling me how to take care of my kid but I also know and understand she teaching me. Dwayne as usual a fairy tale full of stories coming out his mouth on how much he loved me how he would never hurt me well the whole thing was bull shit so as I had said in the beginning November 2013 sai was born shit got crazy I was the one waking up he was lazy when I was pregnant it wasn't much of arguing but then when I had her the cheating began. After all his cheating boom I got pregnant with nevaeh it was hell for me because I was stuck somewhere that I knew wasn't for me but I thought I was trying to make things better I thought he would change after he found out I was pregnant it was bullshit. what choice did I have in the beginning I was sixteen when I first moved in with him my mom never bothered to call the police to look for me she was to busy having her best life my aunt Mara was still there for a little while she was with this white dude, no disrespect not being racist but he was Italian so it seems the same to me so any ways he lived there for a minute until he started that snorting so she had to throw him out the crazy part was me and my aunt spoked almost everyday I had forgot what happened that we ended up losing contact and I just kept doing what I was doing then all this dumb shit start to happen like with my kids father cheating while having sai next to me he will recieve a message from multiple females the part that use to piss me off was that he use to lie and tell me straight to my face that I was lying that I'm day dreaming that I'm just seeing shit when clearly he was sleep and the message came in I looked it up boom what you see a hoe ass braud with bras panties like is you serious I'm sure I said that in the beginning I just like to make sure you get every bit of details.

When I mean details everything Dwayne ain't never helped me when it came down to my kids in the beginning he didn't have a job so he had to ask for money from his grandma or his mom sometimes his older brother just to make sure my kids had diapers like that's mad corny the fact that he couldnt even provide or treat me and my kids right didn't make no sense I never cheated on him even when I thought about it because I was so stuck In love believing everything he told me knowing that shit was all a fucking lie I fought to try and save our relationship because of our kids you want to know how nevaeh came about cool let's begin after all his cheating as well as giving me chlamydia, gonnareah I end up forgiving him we started to be active again and I believe in December is when I found out that I was eight weeks I was excited but nervous I remember that day like no tomorrow I had was just coming from the doctor office I was at his grandma door ringing the bell because I had no keys to that place so either Dwayne opened the door or his brother deon opened sometimes his grandma but that particular day Dwayne opened the door and he looked at me as I looked at him the first thing he said was "what's wrong with you why you making that face? I responded "I'm scared that is why face like this yo we should of never been having sex and I should of got the dam depo smh I'm pregnant and I do not know if I'm keeping it because I can't afford two kids right now your grandma also told me if I ever got pregnant again we both would have to leave just to try and find a room but I don't know smh. "yo you pregnant that's not my kid yo you is a whore I want a DNA test, "Dwayne are you kidding me right now how dare you say that this baby not your when you the only person I'm having sex with don't ever come out your mouth and tell me this baby ain't yours you must be crazy dick head. Mind you I was so pissed off that I was getting fed up with him and being in his presents so his grandma use to take my first born sanai upstairs with her to her room so that sanai can lay down, while I laid on the sofa to sleep because the only thing Dwayne had time for was his video games, calling me bitches or sneaking chicks through the garage like I'm dumb for example he start to sneak this girl name nana like the bitch ain't already know he had a baby mom that bitch can lie all she want about not being in that basement while he was with me but I know for a fact that he had down there I'm just so fed up from this bullshit I can't wait to leave let's not forget on his mom and grandma used me so they can file taxes back just to tell me and him that we had to split 1,000 like wtf was that like that was my money for my dam kids then they was acting like they run shit his grandma was always trying to tell me how to raise my kids and I use to hate that shit because my thing was they are my kids and I should be able to have say so to my kids but it wasn't that way like when ever me and my kids was chilling in the living room the grandma always had something to say I remember this picture like no tomorrow when sanai was born having to live in his mom room while his lazy ass allowed me to get up with stitches and all to grab my daughter he was no good I swear but I also appreciate what his grandma and mom do I just want to learn that's all.

Look at me I was so miserable with him being next to just to take a fake ass family picture with our baby girl sai she was the only thing that kept me smile I love her so much this is my first born she's my everything there's things that killed me inside that stressed me praying to god wondering where was I going to be at in life because there was just to much shit going on in the surrounding of this house the only one I was cool with and she got she left back homes to Brazil was his sister ashley she was to her self she's nothing like her mom she acts more like a white girl but her mom she should be ashamed I remember when Dwayne told me a story on how he came here when he was like two and his brother was like five and his mom left them with his grandma just so she can move to Brazil with her husband and have more kids but when i first came around his sister was around like I said she ended up getting deported back to Brazil because her visa wasn't up to date so they told her she couldn't back to the United States until she was 25 which was crazy to me because she was a good kid she was to her self and had her little friends but the fact that her mom lived a double life was even worse they also have the little boy zaquan that's the other sibling he's the youngest so his mom is with this man name arnald when she already haves a husband she's only legal in America to work but just to be thinking about her mom having a husband in Brazil and how distance they are she have to send money to her husband in Brazil for a couple weeks to make sure bills was good cause a lot goes

On In Brazil she also travels from time to time then come back to philly me and her always was at it like a mother and daughter arguing. I was pregnant with nevaeh and she was living in her mom house still so was I alot of the times she's working or in her room. I was always downstairs or trying to get out of the house because it was always boring in the house.

I remember it got to the point that she barely stood at her mom house she was always leaving to visit her husband ever other week shit was to crazy I was living in a house full of drama i wasn't perfect but how there was I a bad kid i just went through a lot with bad habits I started smoking cigarettes with Dwayne and then I kept smoking so much marijuana that today I still struggle with it I want to fight it so I can quit it but back to what was going on me and Dwayne was at each other neck every day I wanted out I was so fed up so one day I went to my job and called a place I seen on 69 and potter now it wasn't all that cool but it was temporary just to get away from them crazy ass people the place inside didn't look bad it was the outside that was fucked up for example a garage next to the apartment then four more across the street the block was a car lot to me the first night staying there was a little peace of mind and then boom when I woke up it hit me bad because around this time my oldest daughter sanai wasn't living with me because I felt like the space wasn't enough and at this time I was thinking I can deal with just the little one bit things kept getting crazier.

my dad and my youngest nevaeh when I first moved in to the apartment the building was so emotional and so was the people downstairs they was making all kinds of noise then I noticed there was a crackhead above me like I was dead ass scared now I didn't know at first until I start going downstairs to check my mail and there was things missing I didn't put to much attention to it because I thought maybe the mail man made a mistake and all of a sudden the lady from downstairs name shari'ah was saying hi to me asking me how my day was she was even saying my kids were cute because there was times where my oldest child would come over on weekends to come see me and her sister it use to hurt me to my heart knowing that my child wasn't living with me because as a young mother I felt like maybe it was best that she stay with her great grandma nana and I stay with the smallest one until I got my self together anytime she left I was in tears because the hurt I was feeling the things I missed because they had such wicked family mind you my kids are Jamaican I don't have no problem with Jamaican people I just have a problem with their father he was so ignorant that anytime we got in to arguments he would tell me kill my self, my mom a crack head or I would never amount to nothing that hurted me to my heart I ain't know what to do or say besides telling him I hated him or leave me alone I don't hate people I just felt hurt by such words I never disrespected him I always had loved him but when I realized things were toxic I just had to go bad enough before nevaeh was born he pushed me, I tripped over a rug there was a hook literally in my arm I could have died the way it was close to my artery at first I didn't feel nothing because I was mad but when I seen his face of fear I looked down and almost passed out but I knew I had to stay woke that happened because I threw a tooth brush at him for pushing me the first time ugh I was just so glad that I was out of there.

Until six months later I started to experience the worse of my life my lights went out and I had to beg my dad if he can let me barrow a hundred dollars to pay my electric because I didn't have the money for it at this time my money went straight to weed my kids food when they would come over as well as rent apparently I end up having to let the little one go live with her grandma tati because my situation was getting real like I remember when I went to work came home to see my door kicked open everything digged into knob twisted shit was so crazy so when I went downstairs to ask the neighbor did she see anybody go upstairs or did she see the guy upstairs do anything this fucking lady literally just lied to my face that day saying she ain't know what happened she was asleep mind you she had a gay chick in there no offense I did shit with females before but I stopped because I was focus on my kids as well as wanting to be married to a man I did everything possible to chill from shit like that so anyways the lady then closed the door so I went back upstairs called the landlord and told her someone stoled my money and cake in to my apartment they acted like they didn't even care about what just happened so I was up all night looking at the door I couldn't sleep because I found it strange that I leave for work just to come back just so somebody can steal my money like that's weird

After all that dumb shit that happened all of a sudden I was cool with the neighbor after all that dumb shit that happens because at this time I didn't know what was going on so one afternoon I asked her I'm like listen when I'm at work can you look out to make sure no one goes upstairs towards my door and can you start holding my rent money to give to the landlord this bitch was so hype to say yes mind you I started giving her my rent money to give to the lady and at first I was getting rent receipts then boom the recipes I start getting a month later was looking mighty strange so I'm going with the flow and I remember like no more than two months in to this shit I start being stupid again and playing cool with her she start talking about she might need an aide how she can get he worked email from health partners to email me she said they might ask personal questions but I should of known that shit was lie so basically I fell for it the. Strange shit was going on with my social security number there was capital one cards, target cards and Walmart cards I'm like wait wtf so I'm like ok this weird so then me and her daughter Simone got cool at that tome because she would come in and out she would see me with my kids out front or sometimes I would be upstairs in the house we just so happen to start hanging out she was bringing her friend mona around as well as this girl name quana that braud was dead ass simone tail she remind me of the old lady that killed Selena because she was jealous of her now maybe simone did talk about me but I know one thing I opened my doors to her shit got mad real when her mom out her out for telling me that her mom was stealing from me and using my social she even did it to quana me and quana never really was cool with each other because she knocks on my door to ask for shamirah kind you simone told me to tell her she wasn't here so I'm like ok cool chiiild let me fucking tell you this bitch literally pushed me through the door I'm like oh hell nah so she goes to my room just to be like "really shaniqua you got this bitch lying for you saying you ain't here bitch I'm your best friend you don't know that bitch like that." bye bitch go ahead so what like you fake talking shit, so that bitch came in the room with my kid in the living room I had to have shaniqua sister hold my baby because she was there that day so me I'm over here like fuck that I'm swinging this bitch ain't hitting she trying to slap and I'm punching this bitch and me grabbing each other her bitch ass pushed me I fell towards the oven on my stomach this bitch sits on my back then try giving me head lock so I'm like ok this bitch fat how am I going to get up I'm like pause bitch fuck off I get seizures which I do that shut can come at anytime it want even if they removed my tumor so she gets up runs in my room to get the stick in the closet I'm like bitch I will kill you then Mani stopped the fight and shawty left.

    ◦No later than a week I'm at court getting invicted Just because that old bitch was stealing my money and not giving the landlord rent so the man I took care of my best friend he was like a father to me his name was mr Carl he always had me laughing but this particular day I was so fed up so down and tired he said "baby girl what's wrong you don't look to happy today? "pop I'm just so fed up where I live is crazy I want to move I can't take it. Call Anita her ex husband should have something l, the wonderful part about mr Carl was he had dementia but a special one because he still remember me his kids and his friends what hurted me to my heart was I wish I knew my grandfather his younger daughter Bradley had a difficult time visiting him because she lived far but he had an older daughter Anita she use to bring him his food and the things that he needed. I use to look at his daughter like a sis she always tries her best to come when possible. I don't really have a relationship with my mom if anything we talk here and there or she would come over to see my kids when she felt like it but that's not the point the fact of the matter os my mom was always focused on the pass. what about me when I was a kid and I needed you the most you should of thought about that when you decided to take over my ssi but noooo she use to be like she was trying to help me or what about the times I needed money to get on septa pregnant and I'm like 18 and all she would do is keep that money to her self like I'm her daughter I just use to be disgusted by all of it you can't hold grudges and watch your daughter struggle. It was never about me it was always about my brother and his needs if he asked her for food or even about washing his clothes she running to do it even market trips bringing him the things he wanted. people knew how much bullshit I dealt with, my client he was my bestfriend a lot of these agencies do not understand like why hire people when you know dam well a lot of the aides get really close to the patient there's no way that it could be controlled elderly people have this touch that any child wish they could get from their parent but like I said after telling him about my day I ended up having to call his daughter asking her if she knew anybody with apartments or an efficiency room because i was going through things I gave her a small explanation on what happen at the apartment I lived in Anita she told me she will call me back as soon as she find something I waited for like a week for her to text or call.

I finally moved where I live at now wasn't all that cool but it was better than where I was living at before I should of got that old bitch locked up for playing with my identity like that I'm sick I still been trying to dispute that shit for the longest along with student loans it's just crazy I was so stressed I never food shop here I go eat out which is a bad thing but it was because my kids were not here with me it was eating me up inside I couldn't t stand the fact that my kids were separated or they nut ass dad being a hoe and partying it's crazy but it felt so good to be on my own and I knew I was gonna be ok because Carl grand daughters were in the same building but I still wasn't really comfortable I needed my kids with me this shit drives people crazy I started smoking weed every dam day at least like two jars a day sometimes a half in two days but it's only because I was suffering I was hurting I wanted to have a normal life I done been through so much in my child hood life what more do I need to go through I also suffer from depression but I most definitely can control it I had it since a kid I mean like I said on the first chapter I was touched as a kid I seen things no body kids need to see I just wanted to make things right I have two daughters who would be looking up to me.

I woke up in this place it's been like about two months I'm getting ready to take my ass to somebody dam party I follow this group call quiet room that group is crazy but I be seeing that they be having Halloween parties people try to invite me but I wasn't really with it but ill try maybe next Halloween because shit got to real especially with the fact that I live alone I been single for about four or five years ugh I was tired of being alone and bonded a chick was in need but I wasn't trying to be all crazy to much dam diseases out here bad enough ugh g my kids father brought me home stds almost twice every other month so i was not trying to relive that like real shit I don't have time for it so I came up with an idea I got played by a bum why not play these dudes like they played me. Well I decided that I call my old friend from school well I wouldn't say friend because real friends pay you back your money real friends don't hit you up when they feel like it real friends would t be fake well around this time we were friends she was dating this guy I grew up with name Johnny they was chilling they use to pick me up when I use to go to north Philly and visit they would pick me up and we would take the kids to this parking lot in the north where they would play they had this little bar I went in there and got me a shot and I bought some weed from this Spanish boul it was ard to after we got a couple drinks me, Monica and her other homegirl when it start getting late we would go back to her apartment I would chill for another 20 minutes then catch me a Uber as soon as I felt tipsy my ass was going home I kind of was scared to catch the Uber because you got people who's doing some crazy shit not taking organs nasty live shit.

I woke up in this place it's been like about two months I'm getting ready to take my ass to somebody dam party I follow this group call quiet room that group is crazy but I be seeing that they be having Halloween parties people try to invite me but I wasn't really with it but ill try maybe next Halloween because shit got to real especially with the fact that I live alone I been single for about four or five years ugh I was tired of being alone and bonded a chick was in need but I wasn't trying to be all crazy to much dam diseases out here bad enough ugh my kids father brought me home stds almost twice every other month so i was not trying to relive that like real shit I don't have time for it so I came up with an idea I got played by a bum why not play these dudes like they played me. Well I decided that I call my old friend from school well I wouldn't say friend because real friends pay you back your money real friends don't hit you up when they feel like it real friends wouldnt be fake well around this time we were friends she was dating this guy I grew up with name Johnny they was chilling they use to pick me up when I use to go to north Philly and visit they would pick me up and we would take the kids to this parking lot in the north where they would play they had this little bar I went in there and got me a shot and I bought some weed from this Spanish boul it was ard to after we got a couple drinks me, monica and her other homegirl when it start getting late we would go back to her apartment I would chill for another 20 minutes then catch me a Uber as soon as I felt tipsy my ass was going home I kind of was scared to catch the Uber because you got people who's doing some crazy shit taking organs nasty live shit.

As soon as I got in I locked the door took everything off and went and laid down I was chilling I just was bored out my mind but I had to get ready for work tomorrow the only thing I can do right now is blow something maybe watch something on my phone until I fall asleep or maybe I'll call my dad see how he's doing but other than that I'm not really bothered with no body I'm not really in to friends I just got around some people who was ard cool and associate somebody I can laugh with but other than that I'm cool I don't need friends because either they are talking about you or using you and I'm good around this time shaniqua was also staying on and off but end up moving with her sister because of her probation she had used her sister address so she couldn't stay with me.

On may 2nd 2017 there was a party going on I believe this was in down town close to China town inside a little room that looked like a studio I was having fun everybody was cool asf well some of them terry she cool calm and collective she's to her self I ain't know here like that but she was cool and this dude he cool peoples to he ain't never came out of line with me this party they had I think it was in this small ass the one who was running the group name Mando had hosted the party and put music on, it was almost like being in a studio but it was fun let me tell you it was so crazy in that party room there was twerking all this liquor it was almost dam near 2am i was lit like crazy it was already time to go so I asked tell can he drop me off to my apartment on 52nd and market I was lit but I was ok up enough to know what I'm doing I was so exhausted I knew my ass had to get up in about like five or six hours for work.

I decided to get to the house by the time I got in I was so tired I brought people around me who wasn't for me I been looking for peace looking I been feeling pain for so look my heart became way to numb for people I be in my dark clouds trying to look for a light so I can be happy hopefully I can save some money and move so I can really have my kids the way I want to can't wait to find me my mr king someone who can help me with my ways help me with change I lived fast since a youngin so me stripping at a club was something I turn to at one point but it wasn't for me trust me they have some shit in those clubs no body wants to see so since then I been working with mr Carl he is such a nice person mr Carl he be having laugh we be chilling we go get our little snack or lunch and go back to his room and relax but any whom let me get my ass to bed need to get up early once again but it's cool zzzzzzzz...

"Ahhhhhhh I'm so dam tired welp got to be at work, I got to get so much done today at work my buddy waiting for me to get there every morning this was him

He sat down while I cook he would watch his oldies or watch some gospel sometimes I even played some Stevie wonder me and him would clap our hands or sing not a day goes by that we don't be having fun we'll I got to step out the door locking this door making my way down the steps I'm catching my ass an Uber so I can get there because I had to be there by 10am I'm not tired of mr Carl but I'm getting tired of this job it's to much with it the people in the agency treat you like shit they don't care nothing about what you got going on in your life just as long as they got a check.

I finally made it to me Carl he is in bed got to wake him up, "hey pop wake up so you can get a shower I'm about to make you some breakfast to don't you want to go downstairs and see your buddies? "ok baby girl give me about five minutes I'm still tired and I don't really feel good my stomach bothering right now, "pop if you take a shower you will feel better I hate when you don't feel good but I'm still making your breakfast and then I'm going to help you up ok? "that's fine baby girl we can do this, "ok pop so as I begin his breakfast I started thinking about my kids I couldn't wait to see them this weekend I had about four more days to see them they going to come with me to work it's not like I had a baby sitter I did have one name ms gina she was a lot of help she cared if I had to walk Sometimes or she would meet up but I started to bring them to work because i just couldn't afford it "pop come on so you can eat breakfast then take a shower come sit on your sofa so you can get comfortable, "ok baby girl I'm getting up now ohhh kid my legs are killing me but I do want some eggs and bacon, "hey babygirl if anybody messes with you let me know and I'll call my group.

I finally got him off the bed showered up he even ain't breakfast but he doesn't feel like going downstairs, "pop you sure you don't want to go downstairs and sit in the lounge or in the front? "no baby girl I just want to relax in my room I'm not really in the mood to be around them crazy people and their drama I rather be in my room watching the gospel channel. "ok pop I got you I'm going sit down and get on my phone let me know if you want something I'll get up and get it, so as I sat on the chair I saw that I had a message on messenger mind you I'm like wtf is this or who is this so I opened up the message it was another group they had sent to except to be on the group I clicked on it to see what that shit was about yo let me fucking tell you that the group was so open and when I mean open there was coochie, booty, sex videos I'm like yo wtf somebody had tagged me into this post saying post a sexy pic shit the only thing I did was post regular pictures couple people liked it here and there plus I didn't really give a fuck like that I wasn't pressed.

Now we are all the way where I had met this dude named mark and he was cool that night I got drunk I believe we did something I definitely remember protecting my self and so did he I was not playing but that was one time I ain't really like dude he was weird and months later he end up getting with this chick name meanie chick was dead ass weird because all of a sudden she would flirt I'm like nah shawty this chick would have parties some was are until she had her teen cousin there acting like she getting fucked by these people chick was a hoe the last one I went to was ridiculous and I wasn't ha I feel it.

But a blessing happened cause of mark I met his friend he's a little older than me but fuck it he's fine and only because mark was driving and meanie was next to mar and in the mix of driving I'm like who the hell is that old man driving whole time he was fine asf I ain't even know what to say my mouth just dropped I just know that when mar got to park up some where it was a bar by my job so we was in the

Car omg when he instantly got next to me a bitch ain't no what to do I was nervous but they definitely was blazing some smokes and I was definitely with that.

Ones we was done smoking we all was trying to figure out what to do mark kept saying let's go to Fridays so that's when he got out and mark was suppose to meet with him at Friday's this dick head was acting like he ain't want his friend to come to Friday's as soon as we got to Friday's the guy Mann called his phone mark acting like he ain't want to pick up the crazy part was when mark picked up the call the dude man wanted to speak to me I already understood what he meant when he was like I pay her to fuck with me he was only trying to get to know me talk you know kick it shit I been single for about four years hey why not I needed to feel good and he sure look like he can make me feel good his name mann and omg he is sure a man a fine ass one

So mark finally was like you know what fuck it so at first Mann wasn't going to come but I'm guessing he decided to because I was already with them and I'm guessing he liked my vibe and I was definitely with it, he finally arrived like about ten minutes later and he just decided that we all should try and eat somewhere else mark kept saying ihop when we got to the the ihop that shit was smelling like ass in there so picked a different place that they had oh and by the way we in Darby right now and I don't even know this side this my first time on this side this diner look nice looking it's called EMPIRE DINER while all for of us sit we started looking over the menu I wasn't going to get much but I was going to eat shiiit I was hungry after all that riding around crap and so Mann asked me what my name was again I said "my name is Kim but I like to be called Kay. I instantly blushed because I couldn't stop looking at him his lips were so juicy big and omg I just wanted to kiss up on them all I could think in my mind was undressing him ewww father save me he makes me have the butterflies.

As I ordered and finally began to eat my breakfast me and him spoke and definitely decided that I would be leaving with him they must of been mad asf but let me tell you the funny part he slapped my hand when it was time for the meal to be paid for I was gonna pay for my food and I'm guessing the chick and mark thought I was paying for the breakfast they ordered like nah sorry I'm not doing all that I'm paying for my food and the tip my man was like hell nah I got it he looked at mark and was like "yo bro if you don't put some money down these are females the fuck is wrong with you? "Dam bro ok my bad I ain't know bro I ain't have no money I only got the tip money. Let me tell you my boo looked real annoyed but I was thankful he was such a gentleman as we walked out I had got in his truck he had offered to take me home so that was nice of him but them two haters was looking stupid because they swore they was trapping me in to that kinky crazy shit hell nah.

I was to dam happy he had to pull the gas station and he offered me a drink "hey you want something? "sure I take a Pepsi thank you, let me tell you I could not stop thinking about him even while sitting in his dam drunk I sure wanted to touch up all on his fine ass omg. Mark walks up to his window like yo is he in here in like nah he in the store, "yo Mann you got some more gas my bro? Mann reply "yeah I can give you a little something give me a second. I'm like at this point mark was only still trying to be all in our business well to bad sir he gave mark what he had to give him and he came in the truck and we was on our way to drop me off to this crazy ass side of the city which was 52nd and Arch and let me tell you ugh I ain't like it because I didn't really feel comfortable catching a bus or a train so I would catch Uber.

When we finally get to my spot he pulls up and say this where you live I'm like" yeah I practically just moved here because I had a whole lot going on at my old apartment." I'll tell you more about it when ever we see each other again I really appreciate the ride and you paying for my food you honestly ain't have to do that I could of paid for it plus the tip I ain't tripping. "Nah baby girl I don't work like that I don't know what you was dealing with but I don't do shit like that I'm a gentleman you feel me I don't get down like that, "lmao nah I can't judge if I don't know you yet but I sure wish I did because I could definitely undress you I ain't fuck in so long. He laughed looked at me and was like "oh yeah it's like that we will talk about that soon. I walked in front of my gate unlocked it went up to my efficiency and changed my clothes made me something To eat I was so sorry if the long ass day of running around with Mark and his girlfriend but I'm sure blessed to have him to get to know that man.

It was about a week later and we reconnected over the phone he finally came over but what made me laugh the most is when he walked into my room looked around in the bathroom, looked around on my window and asked me was I sick laughed at him and told him "boy you done lost your mind I'm healthy baby trust me. As we did it we started the small something I was making my bed and he asked me how long did I live here around the time I moved here I was already three months in I mean I don't really like it but I have to deal with it for now. The embarrassing part was when he opened my fridge and seen that all I had was juice and water no food no nothing "boo why you don't got nothing in your fridge what you ain't got no money for food or something? "no it ain't that it's just that I don't have my kids right now has my body down so I just don't buy anything and if I do make something I just get what I am making that day eat two days and do it again that way, "this is embarrassing I'm sorry I ain't have nothing here I really didn't want to be infront of mark and shawty talking about my business you see genuine so I'm completely comfortable telling you about what's going on.

"I can dig it you ain't got to be embarrassed about it I just got out of something I was in for 14 years so trust me I can understand I mean I see my daughter but it's the same when you use to waken up next to them you know? "yeah I haven't had mine around I'm about three or four years so much dumb shit my last apartment I was having issues with the neighbor I out to much trust in to her and she stoked from me and had her dumb ass girlfriend going in to my shit when I wasn't home, I can't believe I was to comfortable with that lady being around or even thinking she was trying to help that was one of the dumbest things I ever did. "well babygirl that's why you learn from your mistakes and don't do it again, "let's go get something to eat if you want let's go to a hotel. "umm I mean we can I just don't got enough on me I would have to withdraw some money and then we can just go from there. "That's cool with me ma I'm fine with that we can chill over there I don't really fuck with this side had a lot of shit going on in my life but I won't talk about that right now let's focus on getting the hell out of here.

He took me to the bank we got my money I needed to get out and we was out on our way to the hotel God knows I need this because it's just ugh way to much with all the stuff that's going on I really needed a moment to go somewhere even if it was there to the hotel I don't care I just love his company this will be my first night staying with him in a room alone omg I also love his thought of thinking because he know how important being relaxed is with all the hurt in me this could be fun." Listen once we get to the hotel we can chill we ain't got to do nothing we can just chill I'm not that kind of chick to press a situation like that we can smoke chill laugh maybe watch the or even walk.

"Oh man nah don't think like that if anything happens it's just going to happened with protection until I'm comfortable feel me I mean we friends getting to know each other let's just get the hell out from around here shit makes my stomach hurt being around here." Yeah well we be ard as soon as we leave here boo, we on the highway about to be on our way to the hotel hopefully this hotel haves a hot tub because I need some hot water running on me I really can use that hot water hitting my ass, back and all.

"Oh man this one nice ass hotel I really love this boo I haven't been a hotel since foster care dam that was a long ass time. Omg let me just tell you I'm going in the room change my clothes and getting my self in side the hot tub I know that shit about to straight feel good I just really miss my kids, "yo boo let me tell youI'm liking this hot tub and the hotel it self you really did a nice job. "Thanks baby girl I like to be comfortable can't be sitting around looking crazy

CHAPTER

3

I know this might sound super crazy but now I'm four years in I know seems like wow dam this chick went way to fast with her story but ummm trust my last parts are going to be great first let me start by just saying it took a lot for us to actually be in a relationship God basically put us together because at the time I was already four years in of being single and let me tell you sometimes he can definitely be a piece of work but this man does a lot for me and my kids oh the good part I didn't tell y'all was that I finally got my kids back thanks to God the creator of this world also my boo because if he had not had a court date with his kid mom I would of never got the lawyer that me and him got now it feels so good to have them back I missed everything about them.

I also met his daughter she is so silly she's like a daughter to me honestly my kids her and her dad keeps me going because I remember feeling like I was going to give up but boom I started writing a poem just to get some steam out here it goes I'll leave it here to say my good byes I'll be back with my trust me a lot more here's my poem: my life is difficult in my own world and thoughts wondering when life will change for me when will it be the moment I feel belonged

My life is difficult but I manage to keep strong broken hearts sleepless nights wondering if I will ever make it in life

My life has been a living hell but I manage to keep strong with out consistency and faith life will always be hard

Now I can say my life isn't as difficult because I met me a good man who always make sure I'm on the go with everything I need to be doing we might back heads but let me tell you me and him went through hell and back but I'll get to that on the next chapter

Printed in the United States
by Baker & Taylor Publisher Services